Brian Wildsmith's
PUZZLES

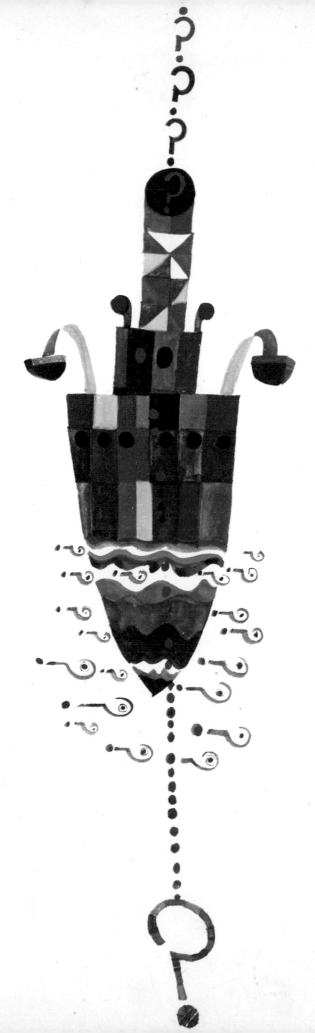

For Clare

Brian Wildsmith's

PUZZLES

watts
INTERNATIONAL

FRANKLIN   WATTS,   INC.,
845 THIRD AVENUE,
NEW YORK NY 10022

© Brian Wildsmith 1970

First published 1970 by Oxford University Press
First American publication 1971 by Franklin Watts Inc.,

Library of Congress Catalog Card Number: 75-125533

Printed in Austria

SBN 531 01550-5

How many chicks should this mother hen have?

What is this donkey carrying in his basket?

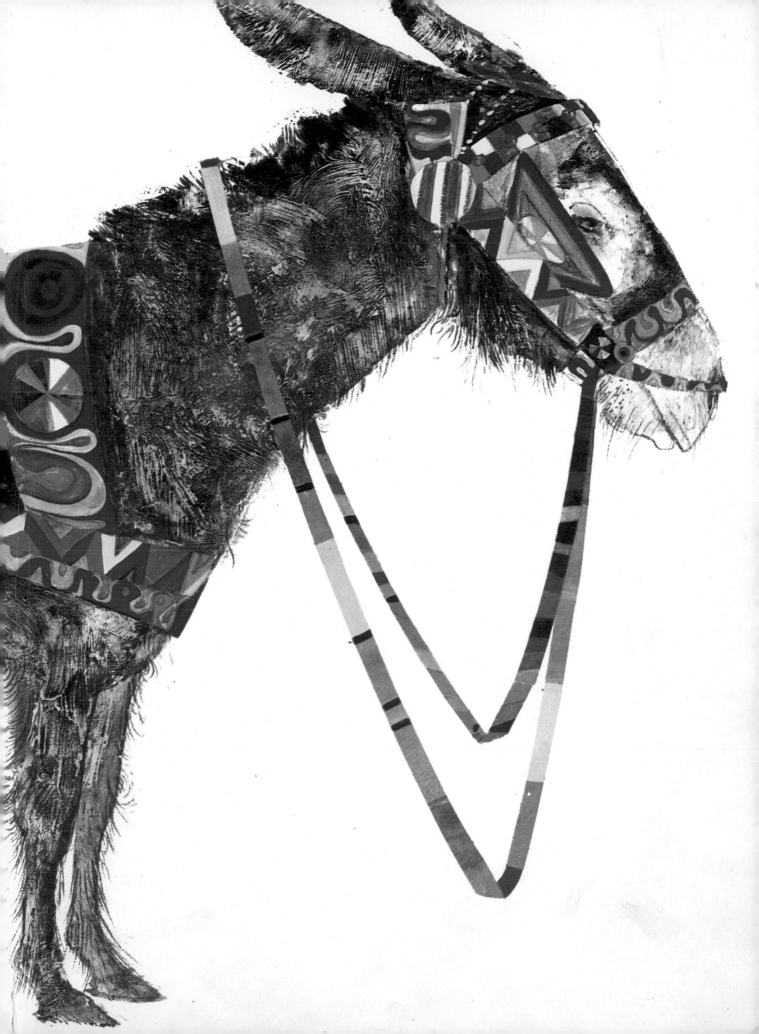

How many animals can you see in this picture?

There are many colors in this picture.
Which color do you like best?

Can you guess what animals these are?

Can you draw their faces?

One of these clocks has stopped.
Which one is it?

Can you tell which
of these three
patterns the
butterfly has lost?

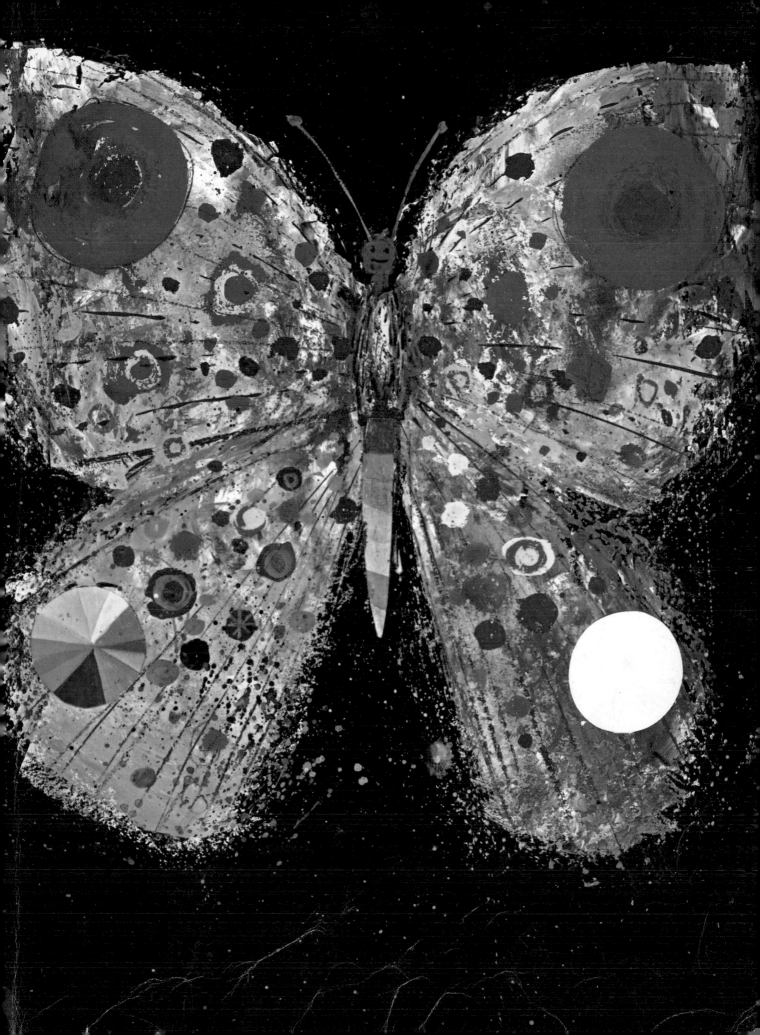

Why are these kittens sitting
under the goat?

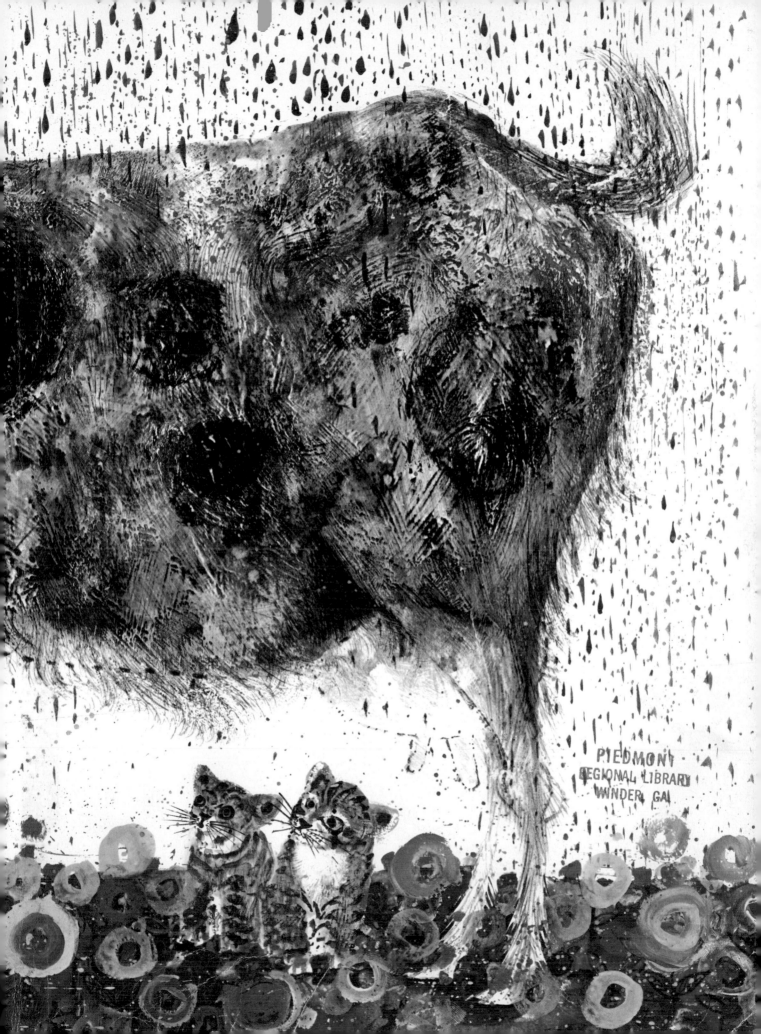

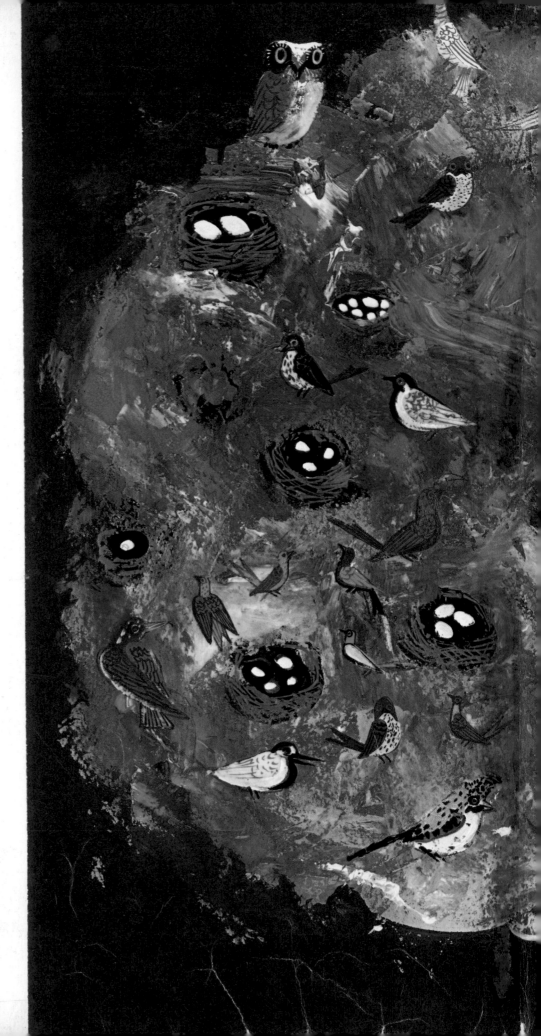

Can you find
the nest that
has only one
egg in it?

How many does he have?

Inside these houses many children are sleeping.

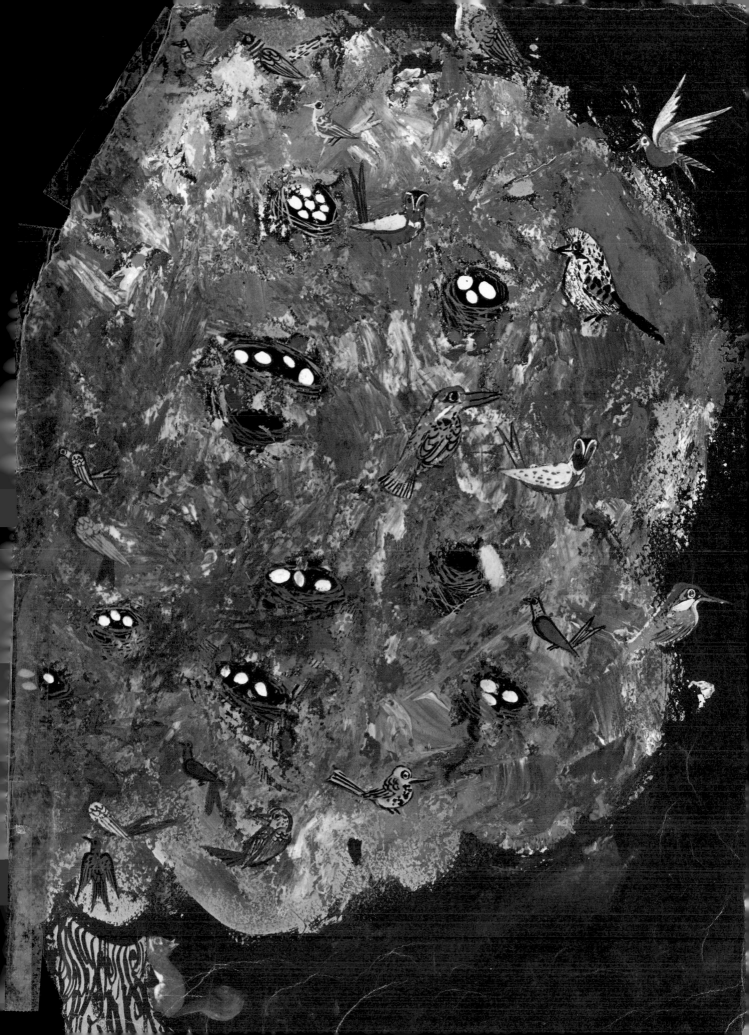

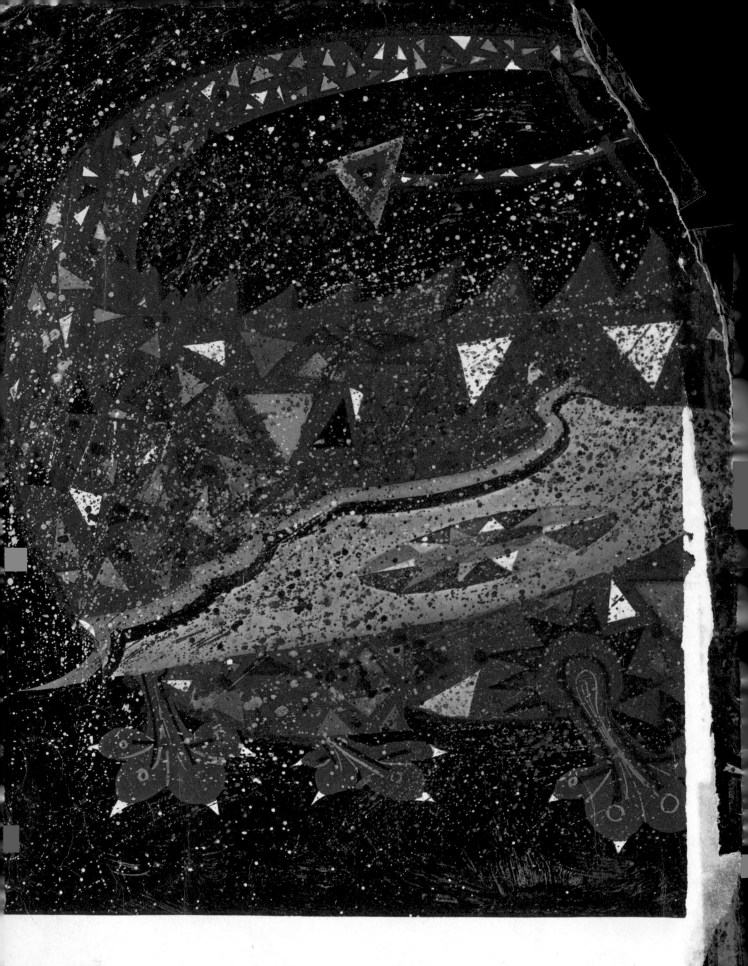

This dragon is showing all his teeth.

Why is this tiger roaring and swishing his tail?

This Eskimo lives in one of these igloos.
Can you find his home?

End . . . . . .